I Love
Baby Animals

Camilla de la Bédoyère

Sandy Creek
NEW YORK

An Imprint of Sterling Publishing
387 Park Avenue South
New York, NY 10016

Text © 2014 by QEB Publishing, Inc.
Illustrations © 2014 by QEB Publishing, Inc.

This 2014 edition published by Sandy Creek.

ISBN 978-1-4351-5532-9

Manufactured in Guangdong, China
Lot #:
2 4 6 8 10 9 7 5 3 1
04/14

All images are courtesy of FLPA Images except for page 48 (bottom) © Rolf
Kopfle / ardea.com, page 102 © Jean Michel Labat / ardea.com and page 103 © David J.
Green - animals / Alamy All images are courtesy of FLPA Images
except for page 48 (bottom) © Rolf Kopfle / ardea.com, page 102 © Jean Michel
Labat / ardea.com and page 103 © David J. Green - animals / Alamy All images are
courtesy of FLPA Images except for page 48 (bottom) © Rolf Kopfle /
ardea.com, page 102 © Jean Michel Labat / ardea.com and page 103 © David J.
Green - animals / Alamy All images are courtesy of FLPA Images except for page
48 (bottom) © Rolf Kopfle / ardea.com, page 102 © Jean Michel Labat / ardea.
com and page 103 © David J. Green - animals / Alamy All images are courtesy
of FLPA Images except for page 48 (bottom) © Rolf Kopfle / ardea.
com, page 102 © Jean Michel Labat / ardea.com and page 103 © David J.
Green - animals / Alamy All images are courtesy of FLPA Images except
for page 48 (bottom) © Rolf Kopfle / ardea.com, page 102 © Jean
Michel Labat / ardea.com and page 103 © David J. Green - animals
/ Alamy All images are courtesy of FLPA Images except for page
48 (bottom) © Rolf Kopfle / ardea.com, page 102 © Jean Michel
Labat / ardea.com an All images are courtesy of FLPA Images except
for page 48 (bottom) © Rolf Kopfle / ardea.com, page 102 © Jean
Michel Labat / ardea.com and page 103 © David J. Green - animals /
Alamy(bottom) © Rolf Kopfle / ardea.com, page 102 © Jean Michel
Labat / ardea.com and page 103 © David J. Green - animals / Alamy

Contents

African Elephant

A baby elephant is called a calf. When this calf was born, members of its family came to welcome it, touching it with their trunks. The calf feeds on its mother's milk, but as it grows it learns how to find and eat plants.

African Lion

Most big cats live alone, but lions live in family groups called prides. The female lions do most of the hunting. They often leave the cubs in the care of the father. Cubs love to play and practice their hunting skills.

American Red Squirrel

A baby red squirrel is called a kitten. When they are born, kittens stay in the nest where their mother cares for them. A squirrel's nest is called a drey, and it is built in a tree.

Arctic Fox

Arctic fox cubs are born in the spring. Their white coats help them hide in the snow, which is still on the ground. As the snow melts, the little cubs grow brown fur, so they can hide among rocks and plants.

Asian Elephant

Asian elephants are smaller than African elephants. Their ears are smaller, too. Elephants visit waterholes or rivers to cool down. They suck water into their trunks and spray it over their bodies. Calves cannot use their trunks at first and must learn this skill.

Bat-eared Fox

Bat-eared foxes live in grasslands in Africa. They dig burrows to make dens for their families or live in burrows already dug by aardvarks. These foxes eat dung beetles, which they listen for with their large ears. Cubs, or pups, love to play.

Black Rhino

Black rhinos live in forests, grasslands, and deserts in parts of Africa. Rhinos are very rare in the wild, because they are hunted for their horns. Young black rhinos are born without horns.

17

Bottlenose Dolphin

Dolphins are ocean mammals, so they feed their young with milk. A baby dolphin is called a calf. Dolphins are very smart animals. They are able to communicate with each other underwater. Dolphins mostly feed on fish and squid.

Canada Goose

Baby geese are called goslings. Adult Canada geese are brownish-gray, but their goslings are fluffy and yellow-gray. Mothers lay their eggs in nests and keep them warm with their bodies. The goslings can fly when they are about ten weeks old.

Cheetah

Cheetahs are the fastest of all cats. The cub's mother catches food for it to eat. Cheetahs live in the African grasslands. The cub's spots help it hide in the grass.

Chimpanzee

A young chimpanzee is called an infant, or baby. Chimp babies hold onto their mother's fur as she climbs through trees, looking for fruit, leaves, and bugs to eat. They are very intelligent animals and can live to about 40 years of age.

25

Common Merganser

Mergansers are ducks. They build their nests near rivers and lakes. A mother merganser lays about ten eggs in her nest and keeps them warm while the ducklings grow. Ducklings are able to swim as soon as they hatch from their eggs.

Common Porcupine

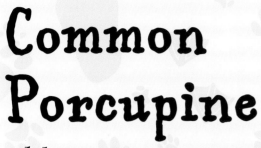

Adult porcupines are covered in long spines, called quills. They use their quills to defend themselves from predators. They can also make their teeth chatter and create bad smells. Baby porcupines have soft coats—their quills grow later.

29

Coyote

Coyotes are wild dogs of North America. They often hunt alone and can chase their prey at high speeds. Coyotes are nocturnal and howl loudly to tell other coyotes to stay away. During the spring or summer, about six cubs are born in a litter.

31

Crested Black Macaque

Macaques are monkeys that live in large groups. They eat a lot of fruit, but also insects, lizards, and frogs. They store food in their cheeks until they are ready to eat it. Until they are about a year old, baby macaques stay close to their mother.

Desert Cottontail

Desert cottontails are wild rabbits that live in desert grasses and shrubs. They can swim and climb trees! Desert cottontail mothers care for their babies in cozy, fur-lined nests. Baby rabbits are called kittens. They leave the nest when they are about two weeks old.

Emperor Penguin

Emperor penguins are birds that live in the Southern Ocean and Antarctica. The father penguin takes care of the egg. While the mother searches for food, the father holds the egg on his feet to keep it off the icy ground. When the chick hatches, both parents care for it.

Fallow Deer

Fallow deer live in large herds. Males grow massive antlers to attract females, but the young, called fawns, prefer to stay hidden. Their spotted fur helps them hide in their woodland homes.

Fennec Fox

This cub may be one of the smallest fox cubs in the world. But it has huge ears, which help it stay cool. Fennec foxes live in deserts. The nights are cold, but the days are sizzling hot.

Flamingo

Flamingos are tall, elegant birds with long, slender legs. A flamingo egg is about the size of a grapefruit. When they hatch, the chicks are covered with thick, gray down. They turn pink as they get older. The food they eat is what makes them turn pink.

Giant Anteater

When an anteater baby is born, it has a full coat of thick fur. It immediately climbs onto its mother's back and hangs on with strong little paws. Anteaters use their long, sticky tongues to lap ants and termites.

Giant Panda

Giant pandas are rare bears that live in the bamboo forests of China. Newborn cubs are tiny, blind, and helpless. They open their eyes at three weeks of age and cannot move around on their own until they are about four months old.

Giraffe

Giraffe babies are called calves. Newborn calves stand up and walk just a few hours after being born. But they spend most of their time sitting in the grass, hiding from hungry lions.

49

Golden Hamster

Hamsters are popular pets all over the world. The golden hamster lives in the grasslands of Syria and Turkey. Hamsters feed on seeds, nuts, and bugs. They live in burrows, where the babies are born.

Golden Snub-nosed monkey

A baby golden snub-nosed monkey has fluffy fur. It lives in the cold mountains of China. Its mother takes good care of it, but its aunts and cousins help, too.

53

Gray Wolf

Wolves live in big family packs that are ruled by a male and female, called the alpha pair. Only the alpha pair has cubs. The mother wolf cares for her cubs in a den, where they stay until they are a few weeks old.

Grizzly Bear

Grizzlies are a type of brown bear. They have enormous paws with long, sharp claws, which are used to dig for food and to fight. Grizzlies often spend the cold winter asleep in a den, where the cubs are born.

Harp Seal

Harp seals are mammals, so they feed their young with milk. Seals live in water, but come to land to give birth to their pups. Harp seal pups need their fluffy white fur to survive in the freezing ice and snow of the Arctic.

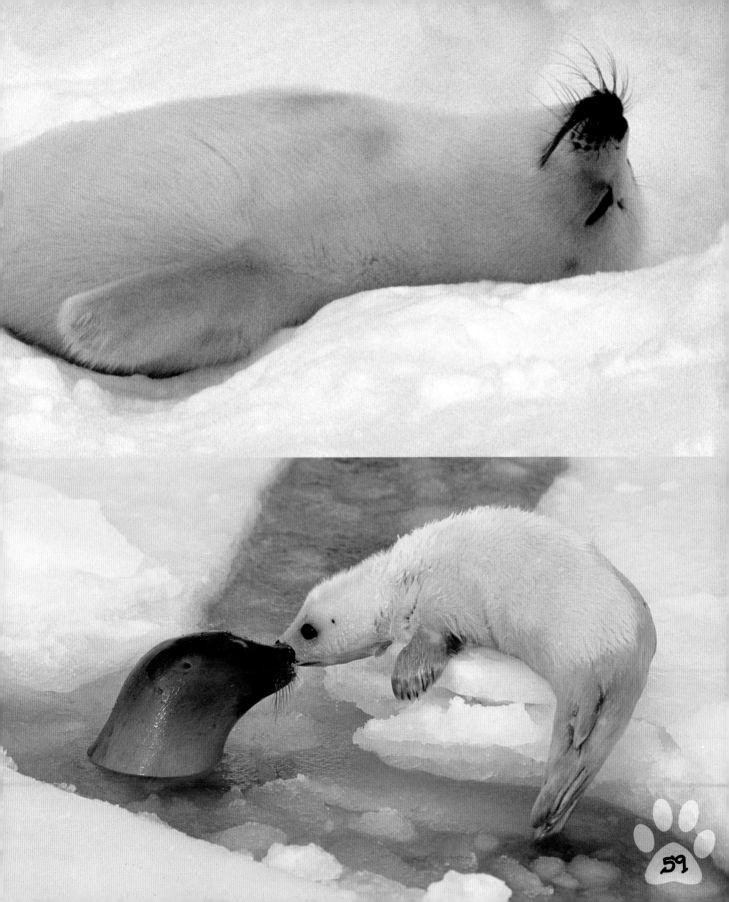

Hippopotamus

Hippos live in Africa where the sun is very hot. They often wallow in water to stay cool. They also cover their skin with mud to stop it from getting sunburned! Baby hippos are called calves. They hide underwater with their mothers.

Japanese Macaque

Japanese macaques are furry monkeys that live on different Japanese islands. The winters are cold and snowy. These monkeys sometimes sit in hot water springs near their forest home to warm up. Baby macaques like to play in the snow and make snowballs.

King Penguin

King penguin chicks do not look very much like their parents. They have a thick coat of fluffy feathers called down to help them survive the extreme cold. When they are three years old, young king penguins grow adult feathers.

Koala

Koalas live in Australia. They are marsupials. The tiny babies grow inside a pouch on their mother's belly. Koalas spend about four hours a day eating the leaves of eucalyptus trees. They spend the rest of their time sleeping.

Leopard

Leopards are incredible hunters with skills in jumping, climbing, swimming, and pouncing. They have excellent hearing and sight, too. Cubs learn how to hide in trees, stalk their prey in total silence, and avoid lions and other predators.

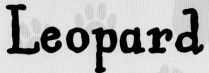

Little Owl

Most owls hunt at night, but little owls prefer hunting in the daytime. They perch on trees, then swoop down to grab small animals from the ground. The fluffy chicks, or owlets, cannot fly until they are about 35 days old.

Lynx

The lynx is a wildcat. It hunts animals such as mice and birds. A group of newborn cubs is called a litter. A mother lynx takes care of her cubs in a den. Lynx cubs have little tufts of black hair on the tips of their ears just like their mother.

73

Marmoset

Marmosets are little monkeys that live in South American forests. They quickly scamper through the trees, looking for insects and fruit to eat. Marmosets live together as families, and often share the job of caring for the babies.

Meerkat

Meerkats are a type of mongoose. They live in big family groups on the dry African grasslands. Both parents take care of the young. Other members of the pack babysit so the mother can search for food.

Mountain Goat

Mountain goats have big, woolly coats, which help keep them warm. Their white coats also act as camouflage. This makes it difficult for predators to spot them in the snowy mountains where they live. Mother goats are called nannies. Nannies and their young, called kids, live together in herds.

Mountain Gorilla

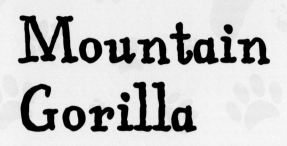

There are less than 800 mountain gorillas alive today. These great apes live in the cool, damp forests of Central Africa. Their fluffy fur keeps them warm and dry. Baby gorillas live with their families where they are well taken care of.

Mountain Hare

Hares belong to the same family as rabbits. Large ears help them listen for predators, such as wolves. Hares need long, strong legs to run from danger. Baby hares are called leverets. They leave their mothers when they are just three weeks old.

Mountain Lion

Mountain lions are also known as pumas or cougars. They are graceful cats that run fast and can leap into trees. Mountain lion cubs have spots on their fur and are born blind. They open their eyes when they are two weeks old.

Mute Swan

Swans are large, white birds. Mute swans are normally quiet, although they hiss when they are angry. Swan chicks are called cygnets. Their parents are strong and can attack predators with their beaks and big, flapping wings to keep the cygnets safe.

Northern Raccoon

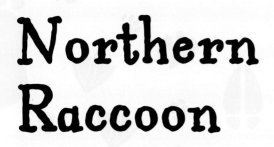

Raccoons usually build their dens in trees and sleep for most of the day. The cubs are safe in a den, hidden from wolves, hawks, and snakes. Raccoons come out of the den at night to look for fruit, nuts, and seeds to eat.

Orangutan

The name orangutan means forest person, and these fruit-eating apes do look like people! Baby orangutans stay with their mothers until they are about eight years old. They live in the rainforests of Borneo and Sumatra.

Ostrich

Ostriches are the world's biggest birds, so it is difficult for their big babies to hide among plants. Instead, the chicks rely on their camouflage to avoid predators. Their fluffy feathers are the same color as the dry soil of their hot African homes.

Polar Bear

Polar bears live in and around the Arctic. They are the biggest bears in the world. Polar bear cubs are born in dens beneath layers of winter snow and emerge in the spring to look for food with their hungry mother.

94

Prairie Dog

Prairie dogs live in grassy places, and dig large burrows. Families all live together. The babies are called pups. When a pup sees a brother or sister they kiss. Pups love to play too.

Red Kangaroo

Kangaroos are marsupials. The mother has a pouch on her front for the baby. When the tiny baby, called a joey, is born, it must climb up its mother's belly to reach her pouch. A newborn joey is smaller than a child's little finger.

Ring-tailed Lemur

Lemurs live on the African island of Madagascar. They belong to a group of animals called primates, just like monkeys and apes. Lemurs live in trees but like to spend the early morning on the ground, sunbathing!

Sea Otter

Sea otters have the thickest fur of any animal. Mother sea otters hold their pups on their tummies as they swim. When the mothers are looking for food, they wrap their pups in kelp (seaweed) so they don't float away.

Siberian Tiger

Siberian tigers are the world's largest cats, but newborn cubs weigh less than a pet cat. Tiger mothers teach their cubs how to find and hunt for prey. By the age of two or three years, young tigers are fearless hunters.

Sifaka

Sifakas have thick fur on their bodies, but no fur on their faces. During the day, they cling to trees and leap quickly to reach new places to feed. Adults can leap 33 feet (10 m) in one jump, but babies are more careful!

Skunk

Baby skunks follow their mother in single file while she teaches them to forage for food. They hunt for insects, worms, eggs, and chicks. Their black and white fur warns other animals to stay away. Skunks can also spray a foul and stinky liquid from their bottoms for protection.

Snow Leopard

Snow leopards are beautiful, big cats that live in Asia. Their thick fur helps them survive in their cold mountain homes. Snow leopard babies are called cubs. They stay with their mother until they are almost two years old.

Snowy Owl

Snowy owls live in cold places around the North Pole, including Greenland, Canada, and Siberia. In the winter, they fly south to avoid the worst Arctic weather. It takes both parents to feed all the chicks, since there can be up to 16 owlets in one nest.

113

Springbok

Springboks are bouncy antelopes that jump and bound across the African grasslands. They can leap higher than 10 feet (3 m) in one jump, which is called a pronk. Young springboks must be able to run and jump to escape from lions and cheetahs.

Virginia Opossum

Virginia opossums live in North America and Mexico. They are marsupials. The babies are tiny when they are born and crawl into the mother's pouch. Baby opossums can use their tails to hold onto branches.

Wild Boar

Wild boars are members of the pig family. Babies are called piglets and have cream and brown stripes on their fur. Piglets start life in a grass-lined nest, where there can be up to 12 in one litter.

Zebra

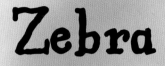

Young zebras are easy prey for lions and hyenas. They must be able to run within hours of being born. They stay very close to their mother's side. Zebras live and feed on Africa's huge grasslands. They live in groups, called herds.